Culture, Customs, and Celebrations in Israel

VOICES FROM ISRAEL

Gil Zohar

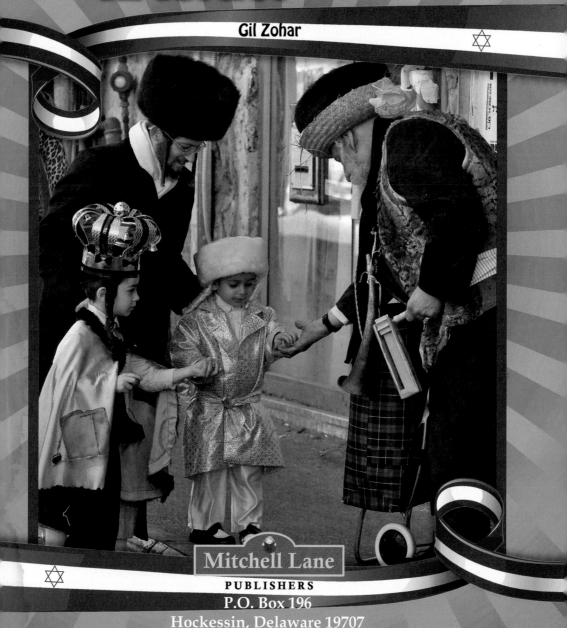

Mitchell Lane
PUBLISHERS
P.O. Box 196
Hockessin, Delaware 19707

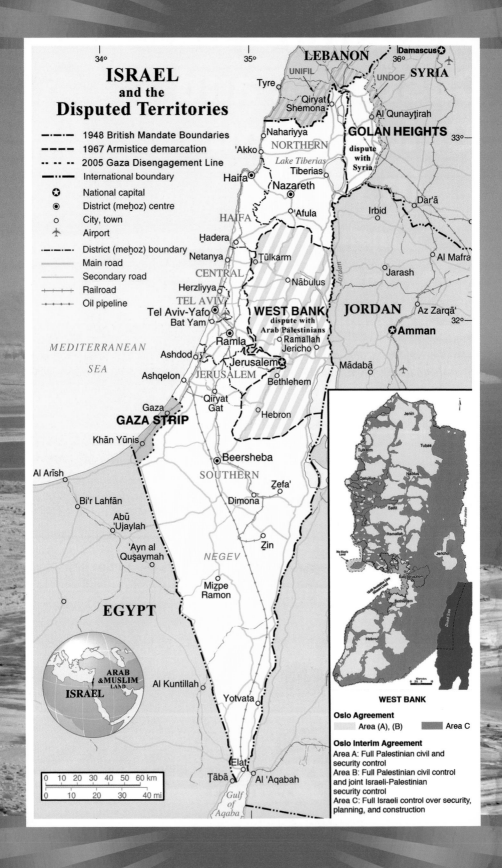

ISRAEL
and the
Disputed Territories

—·—·—· 1948 British Mandate Boundaries
— — — 1967 Armistice demarcation
— ·· — ·· 2005 Gaza Disengagement Line
—··—··— International boundary

✪ National capital
◉ District (meḥoz) centre
○ City, town
✈ Airport

—·—·—· District (meḥoz) boundary
Main road
Secondary road
Railroad
Oil pipeline

LEBANON
UNIFIL
Damascus ✪
SYRIA
UNDOF
GOLAN HEIGHTS
dispute with Syria

Tyre
Qiryat Shemona
Al Qunayṭirah
Nahariyya
NORTHERN
'Akko
Lake Tiberias
Tiberias
Dar'ā
Haifa
Nazareth
Irbid
HAIFA
Afula
Al Mafra
Ḥadera
Jarash
Netanya
Tūlkarm
CENTRAL
Nābulus
Herzliyya
Jordan
TEL AVIV
Tel Aviv-Yafo
WEST BANK
JORDAN
Az Zarqā'
Bat Yam
dispute with Arab Palestinians
✪ Amman
Ramla
Ramallah
Jericho
MEDITERRANEAN
SEA
Ashdod
Jerusalem
Mādabā
Ashqelon
JERUSALEM
Bethlehem
Gaza
Qiryat Gat
Hebron
GAZA STRIP
Khān Yūnis
Al Arīsh
Beersheba
SOUTHERN
Ẓefa'
Bi'r Lahfān
Dimona
Abū 'Ujaylah
Ẓin
'Ayn al Quşaymah
NEGEV
Mizpe Ramon
EGYPT

ARAB & MUSLIM LAND
ISRAEL

Al Kuntillah
Yotvata

Elat
Ṭābā
Al 'Aqabah
Gulf of Aqaba

0 10 20 30 40 50 60 km
0 10 20 30 40 mi

WEST BANK

Jenin
Tubas
Tulkarm
Nablus
Qalqilya
Salfit
No Man's Land
Ramallah
Ne'man Line (Green Line)
Jericho
East Jerusalem
Dead Sea
Bethlehem
Hebron

WEST BANK

Oslo Agreement
☐ Area (A), (B)   ■ Area C

Oslo Interim Agreement
Area A: Full Palestinian civil and security control
Area B: Full Palestinian civil control and joint Israeli-Palestinian security control
Area C: Full Israeli control over security, planning, and construction

Mitchell Lane
PUBLISHERS

Printing   1   2   3   4   5   6   7   8   9

Library of Congress Cataloging-in-Publication Data
Zohar, Gil, author.
 Culture, customs, and celebrations in Israel / by Gil Zohar.
    pages cm -- (Voices from Israel)
 Includes bibliographical references and index.
 ISBN 978-1-61228-684-6 (library bound)
 1. Israel—Social life and customs. I. Title.
 DS112.Z64 2015
 956.94--dc23
                                        2015005451

eBook ISBN: 978-1-61228-693-8

DEDICATION: Dedicated to my wife Randi Zohar, a woman of valor renowned for her Friday night Sabbath table, the fellowship of Torah she facilitates, and her boundless hospitality. Having repeatedly argued with her not to invite more guests than we have space at the table, I succumbed—and bought more chairs.

"And I will bless those who bless you and curse those who curse you and all the families of the world will be blessed through you."
—Genesis 12:3

ABOUT THE COVER: Ultra-Orthodox Jews dress up in costume for the holiday of Purim celebrating the Jewish people's delivery from genocide in ancient Persia.

PUBLISHER'S NOTE: This book is based on the author's extensive work as a journalist based in Jerusalem, Israel. Documentation is contained on pp. 60–61.
    The Internet sites referenced herein were active as of the publication date. Due to the fleeting nature of some web sites, we cannot guarantee they will all be active when you are reading this book.
    To reflect current usage, we have chosen to use the secular era designations BCE ("before the common era") and CE ("of the common era") instead of the traditional designations BC ("before Christ") and AD (*anno Domini,* "in the year of the Lord").

PRONUNCIATION NOTE: The author has included pronunciations for many of the Hebrew words in this book. In these pronunciations, the letters "ch" are not pronounced like the "ch" in "children." Instead, the letters "ch" represent the Hebrew letter chet, which sounds like a "kh" or hard "h" sound, similar to the "ch" in "Loch Ness Monster."

PBP

CONTENTS

Introduction
ISRAEL'S RAPIDLY EVOLVING SOCIETY

Culture in Israel is dynamic. Like in America or in Europe, pop culture, though rooted in history, is ever-changing and evolving. In many countries, culture is influenced by the neighboring countries, global immigration, and military heritage. But in the pressure cooker of contemporary Israel, culture changes more quickly than elsewhere. You can see evidence of this ultra-modernity by the country's almost universal cellphone and internet usage, the high percentage of consumers who make purchases online, and the two-thirds of Israelis who traveled outside the country in 2014. Language here reflects this warp-speed change.

Holidays and holy days in Israel are a combination of Judaism's age-old celebrations and secular Israeli dates. Israel has many festival and memorial days, the result of a long history of military victories and defeats, miracles and massacres, the horror of the Holocaust (1933–1945) and the ultimate triumph of establishing a Jewish state in 1948.

All Jewish holidays are determined by Judaism's lunar calendar. Rosh ha-Shana, the New Year, falls on the new moon in September–October, and Passover on the full moon in March–April. Independence Day is marked on Iyar 5 in April–May, while the day prior is Memorial Day. One week earlier is Holocaust Remembrance Day. The emotionally wrenching juxtaposition of the happy and the sad, and the corresponding festive consumption of enormous amounts of food, are forever Israeli.

Monument to the 1943 Warsaw Ghetto Uprising at Jerusalem's Yad Vashem Holocaust Memorial

The traditional cultures of the Jewish diaspora (Jews who live outside of Israel), whether of the *Fiddler on the Roof* variety associated with Eastern Europe, or less familiar Jewish cultures from Morocco, Yemen, Ethiopia and elsewhere, were rejected by Zionism—the political movement to establish and build a Jewish state in the Jewish people's biblical homeland. Before independence in 1948, Zionism created a vibrant, secular culture reflecting modern European nationalist and socialist movements. This young culture of the "new Jew" was swamped by the arrival of millions of Holocaust survivors and refugees from across the Middle East and later the Soviet Union who simply sought a shelter rather than to build the perfect society.

Gradually Israel's official culture as represented by state radio lost its exclusive stamp of approval. Alternative songs with Middle Eastern rhythms were heard on cassette tapes (before the era of DVDs and MPV players), and slowly became mainstream. TV broadcasting didn't begin until 1966, in the government's futile attempt to protect Israel's official culture from outside influences. Similarly the government refused to permit a concert by the Beatles in the Swinging Sixties. (The Rolling Stones performed here in 2014 to many Israelis' satisfaction.) It took until 1986 when a second state-regulated TV channel was launched, opening the door for today's 1,000-channel cable universe. Today the continued existence of the Israel Broadcast Authority is being questioned as unnecessary.

Growing prosperity has had a lot to do with today's cultural diversity. Following independence, *tzena* (austerity) was not only a necessity, but an overwhelming virtue. Today those hungry times are a distant memory—as forgotten as food rationing in Britain during World War II. Pensioners remember a simpler era when consumers could choose between yellow or white cheese. Today's specialty shops offer hundreds of cheeses, both kosher and not. Ever try gudbransdalen or smelly munster?

Welcome to an exploration of one of the world's oldest yet newest cultures, and certainly one of its most vibrant.

Gil Zohar

Most 18-year-old Israelis are drafted into the Israel Defense Forces. The IDF has played a key role in forming Israeli culture. With both males and females serving together, the IDF is also the country's biggest matchmaker.

CHAPTER 1
THE ISRAEL DEFENSE FORCES—A People's Army

The Israel Defense Forces (IDF), known by its Hebrew acronym Zahal (tzah-HAL), is a common denominator in Israeli culture.[1] The majority of 18-year-olds are drafted: boys for 36 months and girls for two years. Teens compete to be selected for prestigious postings such as the air force's pilot school, the navy's submarine academy, or the elite Intelligence Unit 8200.

The IDF trawls Facebook and other social media sites, looking for braggarts who post sensitive information, whether inadvertently or treasonously. This can result in a court martial, and jail time in *kela shesh* (Military Prison No. 6). Ditto for deserters who go AWOL (away without leave), abandoning their post without permission.

Upon discharge from the IDF, most demobilized male soldiers continue to serve an annual stint in the reserves until the age of 40 (recently it was 55). Women are released from reserve duty after the birth of their first child. The reserves are called *miluim* (meh-LOO-im) in Hebrew, and reservists are *miluimnikim* (mil-u-eem-nik-EEM). The camaraderie that comes from aging buddies in sweat-stained uniforms year after year sharing danger and boredom, sleeping together in a tent or barracks, and griping about army rations is a pillar of Israeli culture. The reserves are a social equalizer where people from different social strata—from street cleaners to bank presidents—share the same hardships.

First-time visitors to Israel are always struck by the heavy presence of armed soldiers and youth carrying guns without any uniform. On Fridays and Sundays, bus and train stations are packed with recruits heading home and then returning from a Sabbath furlough.

Indicative of the IDF's central role in Israeli culture, the country's most popular radio station is Galgalatz (Gal-guh-LATZ), broadcast by the army. The station's youthful, commercial-free formula of pop music, traffic reports, and news makes it a favorite of those on long, boring guard duty. Listening to a radio with earphones may violate army regulations, but officers don't object if music helps a soldier stay alert during a tedious stretch in the middle of nowhere in the middle of the night.

Wanna listen? Visit **http://www.glgltz.co.il/**

Israel's military-drenched culture has invented words for all sorts of things: food, utensils, clothing, etc. A mess tin, introduced during the British period (1917–1948), is called a *mesting* in Hebrew. Zahal has even coined its own slang for an idiot: *dapar efes*. The acronym *dapar* stands for *dirug psychotechni rishoni* (initial psycho-technical ranking), which is a fancy name for the analytical capabilities test given all IDF recruits to measure whether or not they are bright light bulbs. Efes means zero.

Improvisation, problem solving, and teamwork are key components of the IDF principles. It is not a spit-and-polish army. The IDF has few professional officers relative to the number of recruits. Thus young adults are given huge responsibilities, both in terms of the grunts under their command and equipment worth tens of millions of sheqels. ($1 equals approximately New Israeli Sheqels NIS 3.9). This phenomenon of low-ranking soldiers taking initiative and challenging their superiors, described in Dan Senor's and Saul

IDF armored personnel carriers and bulldozers. Modern warfare is asymmetrical, meaning there is often an imbalance between heavy defended mechanized troops and a single suicidal assailant ready to die in order to kill enemy soldiers.

Singer's 2009 bestseller *Start-Up Nation: the Story of Israel's Economic Miracle*, has contributed greatly to the bootstrapping of Israel's burgeoning economy.[2] The management skills learned in Zahal, especially in intelligence units, have led to a nation of savvy, high-tech entrepreneurs.

While Israelis are largely patriotic—and a common phrase is *Kol ha-kavod l'Zahal* (All honor to the IDF)—it would be wrong to imply that respect is universal. Already in the 1948 War of Independence military police were searching for deserters. Some teens today are draft dodgers shirking their military duty, albeit most do proudly serve in the country's defense.

That ambivalence is the theme of the 2014 black comedy "*Zero Motivation*." Writer-director Talya Lavie examines the postponed dreams of female IDF draftees as they spend two frustrating years stuffing envelopes, shredding paper, serving coffee, and fighting off sexual harassment while killing time playing Minesweeper and FreeCell.

At the time of this writing, the issue remains unresolved whether ultra-Orthodox teens will be drafted in the IDF or be allowed to defer military service for studies in a yeshiva (religious seminary). The conflict between secular and ultra-Orthodox, between sacred and profane, between being "a light unto the nations"[3] and "a nation like any other,"[4] remains at the core of Israeli society.

In the IDF, as in the US Armed Forces, soldiers kvetch (complain) about the boredom and the danger, even as they proudly serve.

IDF infantry deployed in the northern Gaza Strip in 2014. Though Israel unilaterally withdrew from the seaside enclave in 2005, the IDF has since fought three mini-wars there in an effort to halt the firing of rockets targeting Israeli civilians.

WHEN THE UNDERGROUND GOES MAINSTREAM

Every city in Israel has streets named for the pre-state underground militias that fought the British and Arabs in Mandate Palestine during the decades before Israel gained independence in 1948. As well, battles and wars are immortalized by street names and highway interchanges.

Together with the omnipresence of soldiers discussed above, one could think that Israeli society is highly militarized. But Israel isn't a modern-day Sparta. It's more like classical Athens.

Here's a guide to some of street names one will encounter in Israel:

ETZEL–acronym for National Military Organization, also called the Irgun, underground military group that broke off from the Haganah (1940–1948).

HAGANAH (ha-gan-UH)—Lliterally defense, underground military group (1920–1948).

HAMA'APILIM (ha-ma-ah-pil-EEM)—The daring ones, the 80,000 clandestine immigrants who tried to slip through Great Britain's Royal Navy blockade of Palestine's Mediterranean coast. Most were caught and interred in concentration camps in Cyprus, then also occupied by Britain. In a public relations fiasco, the British sent the Holocaust survivors crammed aboard the ship *Exodus 1947* back to former Nazi concentration camps in postwar Germany.

LEHI (le-CHEE)—Acronym for Fighters for the Freedom of Israel, also called the Stern Gang, underground military group that broke off from the Etzel (1941–1948).

MACHAL (mah-CHAL)—Acronym for Overseas Volunteers, WWII veterans from across the world, mainly Jewish, who fought in Israel's War of Independence (1948–1949).

OLEI HA-GARDOM (o-lay ha-gar-DOM)—Literally Those Ascending the Scaffold, twelve freedom fighters hanged by the British, most in the infamous Acre Prison, from 1938 to 1947.

PALMACH (pal-MACH)—Acronym for Shock Troops, elite commandos of the Haganah (1941–1948).

SHESHET HAYAMIM (shesh-SHET ha-ya-MEEM)—The Six-Day War, June 5–10, 1967, the IDF's greatest victory in which it conquered the Sinai Peninsula and Gaza Strip from Egypt, East Jerusalem and the West Bank from Jordan, and the Golan Heights from Syria.

On Iyar 5, 5708, corresponding to Friday, May 14, 1948, David Ben-Gurion declared Israel's independence in the waning hours of the British Mandate. The ceremony was held at the Tel Aviv Museum of Art, today preserved as Independence Hall. A photo of Theodor Herzl (1860–1904), the founder of the Zionist movement, hangs on the wall behind Ben-Gurion.

CHAPTER 2

A *Kulturkampf* Over Religion Divides Society

David Ben-Gurion, Israel's first prime minister, envisioned a secular, socialist state protecting freedom of religion in which traditional Jewish life would be relegated to nostalgia.

In May 1948 when the country's founding fathers hastily met in the twilight of the Mandate (British colonial rule) to write the Declaration of Independence, their draft document failed to mention God. The committee's single rabbi vehemently objected. Finally a compromise was reached—and the ambiguous words "Rock of Israel" inserted.[1] Not surprisingly, Israel has no constitution.

That dispute was the opening round of a *kulturkampf* (cultural war) between secular and religious that has torn apart Israeli society ever since.

At issue is whether the 25-hour Friday dusk to Saturday sunset is the holy Sabbath in which one goes to pray in the synagogue, or the weekend to play at the beach. Ditto for Judaism's festivals. Are they holy days or holidays? Time to be with family, or jet away for an exotic vacation? Can businesses stay open, or must they close?

The issue is not black and white. Heading home Friday afternoon, bareheaded, non-observant Israeli commuters wish the bus driver *Shabbat shalom* (Sabbath peace) and he cheerfully replies, "To you, too." (To the chagrin of secular Jews without cars, most public transportation doesn't operate on the Sabbath.) The ultra-religious Jews do not drive on the Sabbath. They must walk.

Municipal bylaws govern Sabbath business openings. Amongst the bizarre sights one encounters here is a store illegally open on Friday night being picketed by ultra-Orthodox men chanting "Holy Sabbath."

Rock throwing and riots over the Sabbath status quo happen frequently, especially during the hot months when some teenagers look for summer fun. One third of Jerusalem's streets are closed to motor traffic by police barriers for the duration of the Sabbath.

Is Israel becoming more or less religious? That's a complicated question. Hareidim (huh-ray-DEEM, ultra-Orthodox Jews, literally those who quake before God) have seen their numbers grow over recent decades; people who don't practice birth control are blessed with large families. But following the 2013 elections for the Knesset (kuh-NESS-et, Parliament), a coalition government was formed that excluded the ultra-Orthodox parties. In March 2015, as this book was going to press, Israelis again headed to the voting booths. It remains to be seen how much treasury funding Haredi politicians and their constituents will now receive. Reduced subsidies for their special interests has forced an ever-growing number of the ultra-Orthodox to enter the labor market and work for a living.

Israel's ultra-religious Jews have been raising the walls on their self-imposed isolationist ghettos to reduce exposure to broader society. While TV has long been forbidden, some rabbis have now endorsed "kosher cellphones" in which illicit sites are blocked. These ultra-religious Jews do not have cars. They are easily identified by their curled sidelocks, which are never cut.

Lalov Chassidim gather at their synagogue in Bnei Brak near Tel Aviv to celebrate the birth of a baby. The various Chassidic groups follow the teachings of a Polish mystic known as the Baal Shem Tov (1698–1760) to spread joy. Their way of life is filled with religious celebrations.

Meanwhile, there are growing numbers of secular Jews, particularly immigrants from the United States and Russia, who are exploring traditional Jewish rituals.

The questions linger. Has Israel's ultra-Orthodox minority lost the culture war? Or will Israel become a theocracy like its Middle Eastern neighbors Iran, Afghanistan and Saudi Arabia? Will Israel become the Jewish State or remain the state of the Jews?

Many Israelis celebrate the Sabbath with a Friday-night family dinner. Though the menu varies, all such holy banquets include twin loaves of challah bread, candles and wine. While some Israelis strictly observe Shabbat, others will follow the ritual dinner by watching TV or driving to visit friends—acts considered violations of the Sabbath.

SHABBAT SHALOM

More than Israel has kept the Sabbath, the Sabbath has kept Israel. *Shabbat* is TGIF–Thank God It's Friday. After a grueling six days of work, by Friday afternoon, Israelis are ready for the highlight of the week—the work-free, no computers, TV-free time-out that Judaism hails as the purpose of God's creation.

While the women are cooking up a storm for the numerous dinner guests on Friday night, the men are out shopping for flowers, wine, and cake. All food for Shabbat must be made in advance. Once the sun sets and Shabbat begins, observant Jews no longer use electric stoves or ovens.

A blaring single-note, minute-long siren—distinct from a rising and falling air raid warning—heralds the Holy Sabbath. The women frantically race through the remaining 18 minutes permitted to finish the food preparations. They then make the blessing over the twin Sabbath candles formally ushering in God's day of rest. Answering "Amen," the men head off to synagogue, where they join the loud singing and dancing. Friday night in synagogue gives new meaning to "make a joyful noise." Everywhere in Israel, the neighborhood synagogue is a short walk away. Most married women stay home to prepare the family Sabbath meal. Those who do attend Sabbath eve services sit separately from the men. Gender separation is common in Middle Eastern cultures.

Returning home after 90 minutes, the men welcome both the regulars and the ever-changing guests. Most guests at the Shabbat table are Jewish but sometimes Christian and Muslim friends, or tourists from abroad are invited.

Before breaking bread, families sing a song welcoming the Sabbath angels. Parents then bless their children, and all the unblessed children of the world. The ceremony continues with a blessing over wine, and ritual hand washing. Finally they break bread and eat Shabbat dinner.

A common Sabbath menu might include soup, salad, hummus and chicken. Sabbath menus aren't carved in stone. While hardly traditional, even sushi can be served.

As the meal progresses, the conversation turns to the week's Hebrew Bible portion. Some like reading something found surfing the Internet or in that day's newspaper. Some consider this Torah talk the main course and the food, however delicious, the appetizer.

The holy banquet continues on into the night, with more singing, words of wisdom, *kibitzing* (KIH-but-zing), and toasts of *l'chaim* (to life).

(If you visit Jerusalem, please let me know. My e-mail is GilZohar@rogers.com. There's always room at my Shabbat table for another guest.)

Among the 1.25 million people from the former Soviet Union who have settled in Israel are veterans of the "Great Patriotic War," as Russians call World War II. Here Red Army vets are seen in downtown Jerusalem after a ceremony marking the defeat of Nazi Germany. In the first three years following independence in 1948, Israel saw a wave of immigration by some 680,000 Holocaust survivors and North Africans which doubled its population. Today Israel is absorbing a wave of immigrants from France and Western Europe escaping anti-Semitism.

CHAPTER 3
A BILINGUAL STATE—
Russian and Hebrew

An oft-repeated joke here is that Israel has two official languages: Russian and Hebrew. (In fact, Hebrew and Arabic are the official languages though English is widely spoken.) Today 1.25 million Russian speakers live in Israel. About one quarter are not Jewish according to rabbinic law. These immigrants arrived here, and continue to make aliya (ah-lee-AH), under the Law of Return–Israel's immigration act which guarantees citizenship to anyone with a single Jewish grandparent. Given the high degree of intermarriage in the former Soviet Union stemming from dictator Josef Stalin's policy of cultural genocide, huge numbers fall into that category.

Food and language often go together. The Russians have brought with them a love of "white steak" (pork), herring and vodka.

Since the Iron Curtain began unravelling in 1989 and mass emigration became a reality, many families with a tenuous link to Judaism have made their home here. They now speak Hebrew, serve in the IDF, pay taxes, and view themselves as Israelis. But their questionable religious status impacts their lives. Since Israel has no civil marriage, they are forced to tie the knot abroad, in Cyprus or elsewhere, and then register their marriage with the Ministry of the Interior.

Russian Orthodox monks visit the Church of the Holy Sepulcher in Jerusalem during Orthodox Easter. More than 350,000 Israelis are Russians who immigrated following the collapse of the Soviet Union and are not considered Jewish by Israel's Ministry of the Interior.

HEBREW—A LANGUAGE REBORN

What of Hebrew, the other half of the above-mentioned joke? Hebrew, today the common language of Israel's 8.3 million citizens, was literary rather than a spoken language until the late 19th century. Itamar Ben-Avi (1882–1943) was the first child in some 2,000 years to speak Hebrew as his mother tongue. He hated his father, philologist Eliezer Ben-Yehuda (1858–1922), who literally locked his infant son in a language incubator to which only Hebrew speakers were permitted to enter.[1] Ben-Yehuda set for himself the task of reviving the dead language as part of the Zionist enterprise.

Filling the lexical gaps, he invented thousands of new words for things like oranges, which come from China and were brought to the Mediterranean world by Portuguese sailors in the 16th century. *Tapuz*, literally golden apple, is so embedded in Israeli culture that many people no longer recognize the word for orange as an acronym.

Ben-Yehuda, not to mention Isaiah or Jesus, would find today's spoken Hebrew unintelligible, even if the grammar remains similar to biblical forms. Slang and invented vocabulary have created a new language.

The Hebrew Bible, called Torah in Hebrew, is the touchstone on which Israeli culture has developed. Hebrew, like Arabic and other Semitic languages, is written right to left. The Hebrew alphabet has 22 letters. Seen here is page 1 of Genesis. The words "In the beginning" appear in bold in the upper right corner. The remainder of the page is commentary.

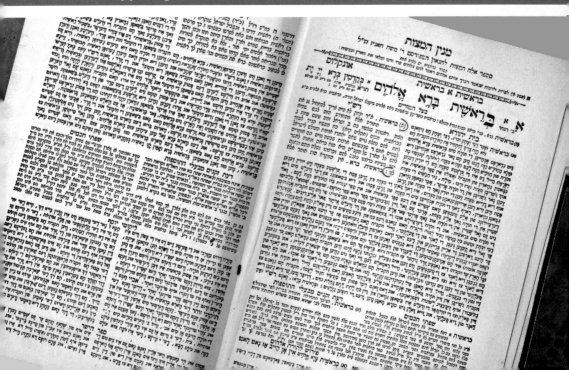

Hannah Szenes was a poet and playwright, writing both in Hungarian and Hebrew. She parachuted into Nazi-occupied Europe in 1944 in a doomed mission to save the Jews of Europe from the Holocaust. Caught, she was executed by firing squad. Szenes's best known poem is *Halikha LeKesariya* ("A Walk to Caesarea"), commonly known as *Eli, Eli* ("My God, My God"). The well-known melody was used to close the film *Schindler's List*.

CHAPTER 4
Song and Dance at Work and Play

How do Israelis spend their Sunday to Thursday (work week) evenings? In its days of innocence, song and dance served the political agenda of Zionism aiming to create a Jewish state.

Although poetess and playwright Hannah Szenes (1921–1944) was executed by a Hungarian firing squad at the tender age of 23, she left an indelible mark on the not-yet-born country. Perhaps her most famous poem is "A Walk to Caesarea," commonly known by its opening words as *Eli, Eli* ("My God, My God"). The well-known melody was used in the soundtrack of the 1993 Academy Award-winning film *Schindler's List*:

> *My God, My God, I pray that these things never end,*
> *The sand and the sea,*
> *The rustle of the waters,*
> *The lightning of the heavens,*
> *The prayer of man.*
> **You can hear it at:**
> **https://www.youtube.com/watch?v=4ZAIPzERkkI**

Other literary figures whose poems set to music have shaped Israeli culture include Rachel Bluwstein (1890–1931), universally known as Rachel, Leah Goldberg (1911–1970), and Natan Alterman (1910–1970).

Moments before Prime Minister Yitzhak Rabin (1922–1995) was assassinated at a peace rally at Tel Aviv City Hall, he recited the poem, *A Song for Peace*. This anthem of Israel's peace camp was banned from state radio when recorded in 1969. The blood-stained sheet with its anti-war lyrics was later retrieved from Rabin's breast pocket. A mournful bilingual rendition can be heard at **http://www.youtube.com/watch?v=aNb2Qsh0F_Q**

"A Song for Peace" was part of a post-1967 Six-Day War generation of music that broadened lyrics beyond nationalism. Influenced by the Beatles, Danny Sanderson (1950–) and his rock group *Kaveret* (Beehive) also sang anti-war hits and popularized love songs with nonsensical lyrics such as "I remember her from the grocery store." While the band broke up in 1976, a reprise concert in Tel Aviv in 2013 drew more than 100,000 people. Listen to *The Grocery Store* at **http://www.youtube.com/watch?v=x6g9kRy5J64&feature=kp** but advance the cursor halfway to skip Sanderson's nonsensical story about a fictional character named Poogy.

Equally popular was Arik Einstein (1939–2013), a prolific troubadour whose death sent the entire country into mourning. One of his many popular songs, *You and I (can change the world)* can be heard at **http://www.timesofisrael.com/arik-einstein-six-essential-songs/**

Born in Tel Aviv's Ha-Tikva slum, Ofra Haza (1957–2000) began her career singing paeans to the Land of Israel but switched her repertoire to fuse elements of Eastern and Western instrumentation, orchestration and dance-beat. Her hit *Im Nin'alu*, setting to music a prayer by 17th-century Yemenite mystic Rabbi Shalom Shabazi, became a disco hit. The poem opens with the words:

> *Even if the gates of the rich are closed, the gates of heaven will never be closed.*

You can hear it at

http://www.youtube.com/watch?v=5px-ppcQDps&feature=kp

HORA, DEBKA, AND RAVE

Israeli folk dancing, including the iconic *hora*–one of the most well-known circle dances, is part of the ersatz Zionist culture that flourished in the decades before independence in 1948. Danced by Zionist pioneers on *kibbutzim* (collective farms) to traditional Eastern European klezmer and folk songs, these circle dances would spin for hours at a whirling, dizzying pace in a joyous expression of life. With each dancer's arms locked around the shoulders of those flanking him, dancers were sometimes lifted off the ground.

Hava Nagila (ha-VAH-nih-GILA), the most popular of these hora dances, means "Let's be happy." The lyrics come from Psalm 118, verse 24 while the song was likely composed in 1918 to celebrate Great Britain's victory over Ottoman Turkey in World War I.

(In 1917, Britain issued the Balfour Declaration declaring His Majesty's government would work to establish a Jewish homeland in Palestine. This document was incorporated in the post-WWI mandate granted by the new League of Nations to Britain. Many Jews assumed a Jewish country would be quickly established. They were gravely disappointed in the 1930s and 1940s when Britain **reneged** on its international obligation to establish Israel as a Jewish state just as millions of European Jews were clamoring for immigration certificates to Palestine.)

Other popular folk dances have been created based upon the Bedouin (beh-doe-WIN) *debka*, and Chassidic and Yemenite traditional dances. Belly dancing by both men and women remains popular among Israelis from a Middle Eastern background.

While folk dancing is popular and dance festivals are part of the yearly cultural calendar, the art form today has lost its predominance. Culture buffs are just as likely to go see a jazz dance performance or the ballet. Discos with pop music and trance raves are the most common place Israelis go to boogie.

Both men and women enjoy belly dancing

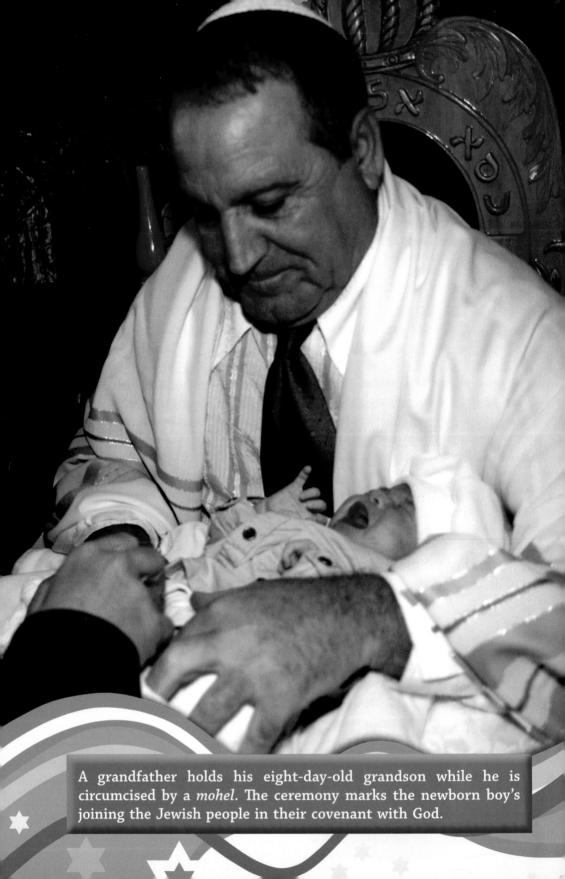

A grandfather holds his eight-day-old grandson while he is circumcised by a *mohel*. The ceremony marks the newborn boy's joining the Jewish people in their covenant with God.

CHAPTER 5
Lifecycle Events

If in America people are obsessed with lifestyle, in Israel life is dominated by lifecycle.[1]

A joke about pregnancy runs, "Boy or girl. It doesn't matter. The main thing is a [male] ritual circumcision." Healthy Jewish baby boys are circumcised at eight days old. *Brit milah* (the covenant of circumcision) marks an infant's induction into the Jewish people. Babies receive their name at this ceremony, and are subsequently registered in the Ministry of the Interior's population registry.

Typically hundreds of family, friends and colleagues attend this joyful celebration, which involves a *mohel* (ritual circumciser) who may not be a medical doctor. The job of *sandak* (godfather) is reserved for a senior family member or honored guest. Traditionally the newborn is placed on a pillow on the sandak's lap while he himself sits on an ornate, throne-like chair. The ceremony is followed by a banquet in which large amounts of food and alcohol are consumed as if to guarantee the newborn a bounteous life. Well-wishers traditionally bless the parents that they merit to raise their newborn to the Torah, the wedding canopy, and a life of good deeds.[2]

Jewish weddings are completely over the top. A small nuptial can mean 200 people. Hundreds more may be invited only for dessert. Like so much of life here, weddings have come to blend elements of Jewish tradition with pop culture portrayed in Hollywood movies and Madison Avenue advertising.

The bride may wear an ornate white wedding dress. Not-for-profit societies loan out expensive gowns at nominal cost

Mazal tov! An Orthodox Jewish wedding. Israel has no civil marriage forcing some Israelis to fly to Cyprus to tie the knot.

to poor couples for their big night, to be returned after dry-cleaning. The groom may wear a suit. Ties are optional, and tuxedos rare. Many of the guests may show up in jeans and sandals.

In a further example of the kulturkampf referred to earlier, many of the male guests will place a napkin on their head as the officiating rabbi chants the traditional seven blessings. Somehow they have failed to bring a skullcap, called a *kippa* in Hebrew, which men traditionally wear to synagogue and at celebrations such as weddings.

What gift should one bring the newlyweds?

The favorite present is an envelope stuffed with cash or a check. It's polite to calculate the cost of the wedding per head, and bring a gift that exceeds that amount so the newlyweds or their families aren't stuck with the bill for an ostentatious party.

Secular couples may honeymoon after the wedding. Traditional Jews prefer to stay in town for a week-long series of parties hosted by family and friends, and infused with words of Torah.

While in America it is considered rude to tell people how many children (if any) to have, in Israel such blunt talk of starting a family is common.

In America, many 13-year-old Jewish boys and 12-year-old Jewish girls celebrate their reading from the Torah for the first (and perhaps only) time with a dazzling soirée held on a Saturday. In Israel, bar and bat mitzvah events are much simpler.

At the age of 13, most Israeli boys celebrate their *bar mitzvah* by publicly chanting Torah for the first time. The Western Wall in Jerusalem is a popular site for these festive celebrations. A teen who has become bar mitzvah (subject to the commandments) can now be counted in rituals which require 10 Jewish men. During morning prayers Jews strap leather boxes by their heart and brain, called tefillin. Inside the boxes are biblical verses about the unity of God.

Mondays and Thursdays—the market days in the time of the Bible—are preferred over Saturdays. Thus no Sabbath violation is caused by guests traveling to the celebration and snapping photos. Jerusalem's Western Wall is a favorite venue for these celebrations. Drummers and shofar blowers dressed in flowing Bedouin robes often accompany the bar mitzvah boy who parades under a canopy to the Torah reading table. For girls, rituals in more traditional settings are still evolving.

Many bar mitzvah celebrations, like this one proceeding through the Dung Gate of the Old City of Jerusalem to the Western Wall, include a troupe of drummers and shofar blowers. The latter one-note instrument, made from a ram's horn, recalls Abraham's near-sacrifice of his Isaac on Mount Moriah.

AFTER 120

In raising a toast, Israelis traditionally wish each other *l'chaim* (to life) and ad *meah v'esrim* (until 120)—the proverbial age of Abraham the Patriarch. What of the final event in the life cycle? If weddings in Israel tend be big, funerals are the same. Attending a burial is considered a final act of kindness to the deceased.[3] All employed or self-employed workers contribute to the National Insurance Institute (NII); in turn the NII provides a cemetery plot to each citizen.

Cremations are taboo. This reflects both Judaism's belief that the physical body will be reborn when the Messiah comes, and a lingering memory of the Holocaust in which millions of murdered Jews were incinerated in concentration camp crematoria. Military funerals are briefly broadcast on TV and radio, and reported on in daily newspapers. The corollary of life in Israel as extra sweet is that funerals are often extra bitter.

Many of the mourners proceed directly from the cemetery to the home of the deceased where first-degree relatives—mother, father, wife, husband, brother, sister, son or daughter—sit *shiva* for seven days. During this week of intense mourning, the mourners sit on low stools or chairs without cushions. Neither shaving nor bathing, they continue to wear the clothes they ritually tore at the gravesite. While observant Jews recite the mourners' *kaddish* three times daily at public prayers for 11 months, others may recite the prayer less frequently. Synagogues are always packed for the four annual holy days when the *yizkor* prayer for the dead and Jewish martyrs is recited.

Jerusalem's Mount of Olives has served as a cemetery from the time of the Bible. Burials continue, and among the graves which draw pilgrims are the tomb of Prime Minister Menachem Begin and Hebrew philologist Eliezer Ben Yehuda.

Hebrew	English	Number	Length	Civil Equivalent
ניסן	Nissan	1	30 days	March–April
אייר	Iyar	2	29 days	April–May
סיון	Sivan	3	30 days	May–June
תמוז	Tammuz	4	29 days	June–July
אב	Av	5	30 days	July–August
אלול	Elul	6	29 days	August–September
תשרי	Tishri	7	30 days	September–October
חשון	Cheshvan	8	29 or 30 days	October–November
כסלו	Kislev	9	30 or 29 days	November–December
טבת	Tevet	10	29 days	December–January
שבט	Shvat	11	30 days	January–February
אדר	Adar I (leap years only)	12	30 days	Febraury–March
אדר ב	Adar (called Adar Beit in leap years)	12 (13 in leap years)	29 days	Feburary–March

The Hebrew calendar is based on the moon rather than the sun, and is 354 days long. To keep the calendar in sync with the seasons, an extra month is added in the years 3, 6, 8, 11, 14, 17 and 19 of a 19-year cycle. At the time this book went to print, it's the year 5775 since the creation of the world. In Israel today both the Hebrew and civil calendars are in use.

CHAPTER 6
A Calendar Filled With Holidays and Holy Days

Recently in a synagogue one man asked, "When is Rosh ha-Shanah this year?" A second man slyly replied, "Same as always. The first of Tishrei." This joke underscores that the date of Jewish holidays does not vary from year to year. Holidays are celebrated every year on the same day of the Hebrew calendar. But since that lunar year is eleven days shorter than the solar year of the Western world, Hebrew dates shift annually on the Gregorian calendar.[1]

While in the solar calendar a February 29th leap day is added every four years, the lunar Hebrew calendar is calculated over a 19-year period, with the leap month of Adar II added in the 3rd, 6th, 8th, 11th, 14th, 17th and 19th years of the cycle. The current rotation began on Rosh ha-Shana (Jewish New Year) 5758, corresponding to October 2, 1997. At the time this book went to print, the year is 5775 since the creation of the world.

THE MAJOR BIBLICAL HOLY DAYS AND FASTS ARE:
The three pilgrimage festivals in ancient times: Passover (Nissan 14-21) celebrates the Exodus from slavery in ancient Egypt. Almost all Israeli Jews gather with their family for a ritual banquet called a Seder
Shavuot or Pentecost (Sivan 6) marks the date the Children of Israel received the Torah at Mount Sinai

Most Jewish Israelis celebrate Pesach (Passover) with their family at a ritual banquet called a seder. The holiday recalls the liberation from slavery in Egypt some 3,300 years ago. Typically the dinner can last till 1 A.M. or later.

Sukkot or Tabernacles (Tishrei 15-21) is when many Israelis build sheds covered with palm thatch marking the 40 years the Children of Israel wandered in the Sinai Desert

Rosh ha-Shanah, the New Year, and Yom Kippur, the Day of Atonement (Tishrei 1-2 and 10) are the holiest days of the year. Yom Kippur is the only statutory day when all businesses close. Ben-Gurion Airport, tiny Israel's main gateway to the rest of the world, shuts down. So do border crossings to Egypt and Jordan. (Israel remains technically in a state of war with neighboring Syria and Lebanon and one can't readily cross those borders anyway.)

Tisha b'Av (Av 9) is a day of national mourning for the two ancient Temples in Jerusalem. The First Temple was destroyed in 586 BCE. The Second Temple was destroyed in 70 CE.

Purim (Adar 15 or Adar II 15 in a leap year) recounts the Jewish people's dramatic rescue from genocide in ancient Persia by Queen Esther and her uncle Mordechai (moor-duh-KHYE). See Craft Project on page 39.

THE MINOR BIBLICAL FESTIVE DAYS ARE:
Tu b'Shvat, arbor/Earth day (Shvat 15)
Tu b'Av, sweetheart's day (Av 15)

THE MAJOR POST-BIBLICAL HOLIDAYS ARE:
Chanukah (Cheshvan 25 to Tevet 2) during which city
   streets are decorated with lights
Lag b'Omer (Iyar 18) when children of all ages light
   bonfires

THE MODERN ISRAEL HOLIDAYS ARE:
Holocaust Memorial Day (Nissan 28)
Rememberance Day for IDF fallen soldiers (Iyar 4)
Independence Day (Iyar 5)

Places of entertainment close on Remembrance Day when Israelis stand in solemn silence as sirens wail throughout the country for two minutes. In 2014, the country commemorated the 23,169 soldiers and 2,495 terror victims who have fallen throughout the history of Israel and the pre-state Zionist movement. Many watched the somber national memorial ceremony at Jerusalem's Western Wall broadcast on TV. Some 1.5 million came to mourn privately at Mount Herzl in Jerusalem, and Israel's 43 other military cemeteries.

To this list one may add a slew of secondary, non-statutory holidays including Jerusalem Unification Day (Iyar 28), Mimouna

Children putting on a Shavuot (Feast of Weeks) school performance. The holiday commemorates God's giving of the Torah to the Israelites at Mount Sinai. As well, it marks the first harvest.

A Muslim family in Lakiya, a Bedouin village in the Negev Desert, enjoy an array of traditional salads and barbequed freshly slaughtered lamb during Eid al-Adha. The religious festival, meaning the Feast of the Sacrifice, is celebrated by both Muslims and Druze. The holiday honors Abraham's willingness to sacrifice his son Ishmael. 200,000 Bedouin live in towns and cities Israel has built for them.

On Lag b'Omer kids of all ages light bonfires. The holiday, the 33rd day of the 49-day period between Pesach and Shavuot, marks the anniversary of the death of the second century mystic Rabbi Shimon bar Yochai. Hundreds of thousands of people flock to his tomb at Meron.

ברוכים הראים לונדם חג ה"סיגד"

Israel's 125,000 Ethiopian Jews celebrate Sigd. The festival once marked their hope to return to Israel. Since the mass aliya of Ethiopian Jews in recent decades, the holiday has taken on an extra meaning of thanksgiving.

(Nissan 22) celebrated by Moroccan Jews, and Sigd (Cheshvan 29) observed by Ethiopian Jews. Every new moon is a mini-celebration which some women observe.

Many of these holidays are clustered together in the early fall and spring. During these two periods many offices shut down. Ever try to get any business done in America during the week between Christmas and New Year's? It's the same here when people tell you, "After the holidays."

To the above list one can add New Year's Eve (December 31), known by its European moniker Sylvester by secular Israelis looking to party, and May Day (May 1), the worker's holiday—a vestige of Israel's founding socialist beliefs.

While three quarters of Israelis celebrate the Jewish holidays detailed above, the rest of the country is divided into many Christian, Muslim, and Druze denominations, each with its own holy days. For example, Protestants and Roman Catholics celebrate Christmas on December 25, Eastern Orthodox on January 6, and Armenians on January 19.

Muslims, likes Jews, have a lunar calendar so holiday dates are always changing, slipping some 11 days annually. The major celebration is the holy month of Ramadan when Muslims fast from sunrise to sunset. Eid al-Adha marks Abraham's near sacrifice of his son Ishmael. It is calculated it will fall September 23, 2015 (the year 1436 in the Islamic calendar), September 11, 2016 (1437), and September 1, 2017 (1438).

In addition to Eid al-Adha, Druze also celebrate the birthdate of the Prophet Jethro, who was Moses' father-in-law. Called an-Nabi Shuayb, the four-day holiday starts April 24. The first day is only for religious Druze initiated into their faith's secrets. The next three days are celebrated by the entire community.

PURIM CRAFT PROJECT

Purim is Israel's most fun holiday. It recounts the Jewish people's dramatic rescue from genocide in ancient Persia by Queen Esther and her uncle Mordechai (moor-duh-KHYE). Like Halloween or Mardi Gras, children and many adults dress up in costumes. For one day, the world is turned on its head, and making fun of everything is permissible.

Your assignment: create a costume that's as imaginative as possible. You might wish to pair with a friend as a cowboy and Indian, a fireman and a flame, or a policeman and a criminal.

Bring a noisemaker such as a bell, whistle or castanets.

Print (or use an electronic version of) the Book of Esther, also called the *megilla* (scroll) from http://www.mechon-mamre.org/p/pt/pt3301.htm

Highlight the word "Haman," the villain of the story, and each time it appears, go crazy making noise to drown out his name.

Read a chapter from the book. Ideally this rather loud ritual should be carried out close to the day of Purim itself. Those who wish to may attend a synagogue in your city in costume, with their copy of the Book of Esther and noisemaker. No matter what you wear, you'll fit right in.

Purim begins in the evening of March 23, 2016, March 11, 2017, February 29, 2018 and March 20, 2019.

Kids enjoy dressing up for Purim

A set of tzitziot, eight fringes or "tassels" on a prayer shawl two of which are dyed blue using a rare dye produced from the Murex trunculus snail. As the Jews were driven into exile, they lost the ancient dyeing technology which has only been re-discovered in recent decades.

CHAPTER 7

Desert Factory Revives the Lost Commandment of Snail Dyeing

"God said to Moses saying speak to the Children of Israel and bid them that they make fringes on the corners of their garments throughout their generations, and that they put upon the fringe (tzitzit) of each corner a thread of blue (tekhelet). And it shall be for you as a fringe, that you may look upon it and remember all the commandments of God, and do them. . . ."
—Numbers 15:37-39

Joel Guberman has a colorful story in hues of royal purple and brilliant blue. In an industrial zone in the Judean Desert east of Jerusalem, this New Jersey-born occupational therapist is engaged in a halachic revolution—getting Jews to adopt the lost commandment of wearing of blue *tzitziot*. (The Jews believe the fringe (tassels) worn over men's pants tops is a constant reminder of our obligation to God and our fellow man. While no man is perfect, the tassels help us lead a good life.)

Guberman is an expert on *tekhelet*—the little understood dye referred to 48 times in the Hebrew Bible that colored the four tassels attached to Jewish ritual prayer shawls.

Long before Diaspora Jews came to specialize in the *shmatta* business, they had a historic connection to dyeing textiles. One of the Torah's 613 commandments is to incorporate an azure thread among the *tzitzit* as a conspicuous reminder of the complete system of divine rules. That single blue thread and three white ones are folded so as to appear as eight strings in each of the four corners of both the tallit (prayer shawl) and the *arba kanfot* undergarment.

Guberman explains the famous medieval commentator Rashi interpreted the word *tzitzit* as having the numerical value of 600. Together with eight threads of each tassel and the five sets of knots, the sum totals 613.

Historically, Israel's blue and white flag was designed to represent the traditional colors of the prayer shawl and these tzitziot.

Archaeological remains of dyeing vat complexes and vast mounds of snail shells found along the eastern Mediterranean coast attest to the lucrative ancient technology of tekhelet. A rare species of sea snail generated huge wealth for the ancient peoples of Judea and Phoenicia—today's Israel and Lebanon.

Eager to control this source of revenue, the Roman Empire restricted the wearing of royal purple and tekhelet blue to aristocracy, and made the manufacture of these dyes a monopoly of imperial dye houses. The laws drove the tekhelet industry underground, just as other restrictive policies encouraged the Jews to emigrate. By the time of the Arab conquest of the Land of Israel in 638 CE, the technology was lost. As a result, Jews began wearing plain white tzitziot.

All that has been slowly changing thanks to the efforts of Ptil Tekhelet, the Association for the Promotion and Distribution of Tekhelet, which Guberman co-founded in 1993 together with Dr. Ari Greenspan, Baruch Sterman, who holds a doctorate in physics, and Rabbi Eliyahu Tavger.

Their non-profit foundation is based on research in the 1980s of Otto Elsner, a chemist at Ramat Gan's Shenkar College of Engineering and Design. Elsner discovered that when a solution of the purple dye made from the hypobranchial gland of the *Murex trunculus* snail is exposed to the sun's ultraviolet rays, it turns a rich shade of blue.

Making that information widely known and accepted has been a slow process.

According to the Talmud, tekhelet is an azure dye produced from a sea creature known as a *chilazon*. Rabbinic sages ruled that vegetable indigo dyes were unacceptable. Over the past 150 years, several marine creatures were proposed for reviving the biblical process of dyeing the tassels. Israel's first chief rabbi, Isaac Herzog, believed that the violet pelagic snail, *Janthina janthina*, was the source of tekhelet. Another theory was proposed by Rabbi Gershon Hanokh Leiner, known as the Radzyner Rebbe. He produced blue dye from the black ink of the *Sepia officinalis*, the common cuttlefish. But chemical analysis identified his dye as Prussian blue, an inorganic synthetic color derived from iron filings and not from the squid itself.

That dispute continues to reverberate until today. Much of the blue-colored tzitziot worn in Israel today are dyed from the inexpensive cuttlefish.

How mainstream is the wearing of tekhelet?

"It's definitely becoming more and more popular," observes Rabbi Avi Berman, director-general of the Orthodox Union in Jerusalem. "Everyone is hoping one day we will know for sure what the right tekhelet is so we can fulfill the biblical commandment."[1]

Berman himself does not wear tekhelet. Instead, he follows the ruling of the late Chief Sephardi Rabbi of Israel, Mordechai Eliahu, that pending the coming of the Messiah, there cannot be complete certainty of which sea creature constitutes the chilazon.

The Murex trunculus snail is found across the Mediterranean Sea

While rabbis tend to be tradition-bound and reluctant to adopt change, tekhelet has become popular among nationalist youth and those living in Judea and Samaria, notes Guberman.

"One hundred percent is a big number," he says of the ever-increasing number of Israelis wearing blue ritual fringes produced from the *Murex trunculus*. "We believe it is a process how halacha gets accepted. Nowhere in the Torah does it say that the tekhelet [source] was a mollusk. But nowhere in the Torah does it say gold is a metal. It's a given."

Today, the Ptil Tekhelet foundation sells some 800 sets of tzitziot monthly.[2] The process requires more than a ton annually of Murex trunculus, most of which Guberman imports from Croatia.

The fringes sell for between $20 to $50, depending on the length and thickness of the string. They are spun on site using merino sheep wool.

"We're the only place in the world doing this from the Murex trunculus," Guberman notes with pride.

What of the future?

Ptil Tekhelet is looking for an investor to establish a snail farm at either Mikhmoret or Eilat. When that happens Israel will have a new, if non-kosher, export delicacy—escargot.

FASHION?
WHAT FASHION?

Writing about fashion in Israel can be misleading. The country has produced some notable couturiers and designers. Among them was Leah Gottlieb (1918–2012). A Holocaust survivor, she founded the glamorous Gottex bathing suit company. Her life and swimwear were celebrated in 2013 at a posthumous exhibit at the Design Museum in Holon.[3]

Still, semi-formal attire in Israel often consists of a simple shirt and pants for men, and a plain dress and sandals for women. Although there is a burgeoning fashion industry, with exports of supermodels like Bar Rafaeli and Gal Gadot, and high-end designers such as Alon Livne, who has designed for the likes of Lady Gaga and Beyonce, there is also a relaxed, "anything goes" fashion rule. In Israel, you can wear almost anything, almost anywhere, except in the most religious neighborhoods and ritual sites, where modest full-length sleeves and dresses below the knees are standard.

Olives and olive oil form
a big part of the Israeli diet

Agriculture is Israel is highly mechanized
but traditional methods are still used. Here
an Arab farmer and his donkey are turning
a millstone to crush olives and
squeeze out their olive oil.

Farmers spread a tarpaulin under an olive tree and then beat the branches to get the fruit to fall. The olives are then pressed at an olive mill. The first pressing results in virgin olive oil. The pulp is then heated in subsequent pressings, producing an oil considered inferior in quality.

CHAPTER 8
Every Day is a Feast Day in the Holy City

Seven decades ago, when Israel was a brand-new state, people here could barely feed themselves. That time of rationing, euphemistically called *tzena*—meaning austerity but really connoting near starvation—is practically forgotten.

Tastes have evolved dramatically as the country has prospered. While olives are one of Israel's blessed seven species of fruits and vegetables mentioned in the Bible,[1] olive oil was largely absent from the Israeli diet until the 1980s. Writer Joan Nathan, whose 1975 cookbook *The Flavor of Jerusalem* was based on dozens of local recipes and lore, doesn't mention this Mediterranean liquid gold.

Today, Israelis appreciate the olive oil-drenched richness of Arab cuisine, even if the political chasm between Jews and Palestinians remains unbridged. As detailed in *The Culinary Story of Jerusalem* by Tali Friedman, and *Jerusalem: A Cookbook* by Yotam Ottolenghi and Sami Tamimi, what lovers of good food find so appealing about the local food scene is its sheer variety. Thanks to Israel's ingathering of the exiles, visitors can sample authentic and delicious cuisine from places you may never have heard of—such as Tashkent, Tikrit, Sanaa, Fez or Gondar. Many but not all of Jerusalem's eateries are kosher; similarly many are hole-in-the wall bargains.

You might start with *sabich*. This stuffed pita sandwich is bursting with slices of Iraqi-style fried eggplant, hard-boiled eggs, hummus, diced cucumber and tomatoes, and pickles. It's

topped with *umba*, a lip-smacking pickled mango sauce. Try it at ha-Sabichiyya, where the unflappable owner Yigal serves up a smile along with the only item on his menu. The line snaking along Shammai Street in downtown Jerusalem attests to his success.

sabich

Meurav yerusahalmi, a mix of organs griddled with onions and Middle Eastern spices, is available stuffed in a pita or as an entrée served with salad and rice or chips. It's the house specialty at Chatzot on Agrippas Street.

meurav yerusahalmi

Hummus, falafel, shawarma, and jachnun, respectfully from Lebanon, Egypt, Turkey and Yemen, are Israeli staples. While fans argue about where to get the best puree of chickpeas, tehina, garlic and lemon, you must not leave Jerusalem without wiping your bowl clean at Hummus Pinati on King George

Street. In the Old City, two of the best known hummus joints are Lina and Abu Shuqri. Ask any local for directions.

In Paris, a gourmand would never walk down a boulevard munching on a baguette. But here, favorite breads are enjoyed in the street fresh from the bakery oven. The only-in-Jerusalem specialty *beigeleh*, not to be confused with bagels from Brooklyn, is shaped like an elongated bagel on steroids. Coated in sesame seeds, they are sold by cart vendors throughout the Old City. Make sure to ask for a packet of *za'atar*, a tangy condiment blending oregano and hyssop.

An Ashkenazi Jewish grandmother might look askance at Kurdish *kubbeh*, but this soup is another Jerusalem classic. Minced meat-stuffed bulgur and semolina dumplings float in a tangy broth of beets and root vegetables. Try it at Mordoch on Agrippas Street or Ta'ami on Shammai. At these high turnover

kubbeh

eat-and-run establishments don't even think of enjoying a leisurely coffee after your meal.

Part of the pleasure of eating in Jerusalem is its connection to the cycles of the seasons and religions. Sabbaths are made

beigeleh

hummus

sufganiyot

rugelach

sweeter with twin challahs or divine *rugelach*, rolled pastries loaded with chocolate or cinnamon filling. During Islam's holy month of Ramadan, when Muslims observe a dawn-to-dusk fast, try *kataif*—crescent-shaped deep-fried pancakes stuffed with cheese or walnuts and drizzled with rosewater syrup.

Malabi is a blancmange, almond-and-rosewater pudding popular in Jerusalem's Jewish and Arab neighborhoods during the long summer months. Conversely *sahlab*, a hot, gelatinous pudding-drink made from orchid tubers, usually topped with pistachios and cinnamon powder, is available in Jerusalem's brief rainy winter.

Sufganiyot (jelly donuts) are another seasonal treat. Cooked in oil during Chanukah in the short days of winter, they symbolize the miracle of the small cruse of olive oil that burned for eight days in the Temple of yore. *Knafeh nablusiya*, a treat popular among both Arabs and Jews, is made of shredded phyllo dough, goat cheese and pistachios. At the Eiffel Bakery, on Sultan Suleiman Street opposite the Old City's Damascus Gate, you may be the only tourist the friendly proprietors have seen all day. Or even all week.

At Purim, everyone gorges on *oznei Haman*, called *hamantaschen* in Yiddish. The triangle-shaped pastries are stuffed with poppy seed, prunes or jam.

One traditional Jewish cuisine is almost entirely missing in Israel: delis serving heaping pastrami and corned beef sandwiches like those in New York's Lower East Side or Los Angeles' Fairfax Avenue are nowhere to be found.

When Jerusalem's 850,000 residents aren't engaged in prayer or fasting, then they're often eating. Start a preemptory diet now. And don't say you haven't been forewarned about the dangers of the Middle East . . . to your waistline.

PURIM HAMANTASCHEN

Purim cookies, called Oznei Haman in Hebrew, and Hamantashen in Yiddish, are made from Prune butter or sweetened poppy seed. They are traditional fillings but you can use any jam or preserves.

Ingredients
4 eggs
1 cup sugar
½ cup oil
juice of one lemon
rind of 1 lemon, grated
1 teaspoon vanilla extract
5 cups flour
2 teaspoons baking powder

Fillings
1 pound prepared filling, such as poppy seed, lekvar (prune butter) or strawberry or apricot preserves

Directions
1. Preheat oven to 350° Fahrenheit/180° degrees Celsius
2. Grease cookie sheets.
3. Beat eggs and sugar. Add remaining ingredients, and mix well. Divide into four parts.
4. Prepare dough of your choice. Divide into four portions
5. On a floured board roll out each portion to about ⅛-inch thick. Using a round biscuit or cookie cutter cut 3-inch circles.
6. Place ½ to ⅔ teaspoon of desired filling in the center of each circle.
7. To shape into triangle, lift up right and left sides, leaving the bottom down and bring both side to meet at the center above the filling.
8. Bring top flap down to the center to meet the two sides. Pinch edges together.'
9. Place on grease cookie sheet 1 inch apart and bake at 350° F/180° C preheated oven for 20 minutes.

Reprinted with permission from *Spice and Spirit, The Complete Kosher Jewish Cookbook*, published by Lubavitch Women's Cookbook Publications.

CHAPTER NOTES

Chapter 1: The Israel Defense Forces—A People's Army

1. Martin van Crefeld, *The Sword and the Olive: A Critical History of the Israeli Defense Force* (New York, Public Affairs), 2003, p. 99.

2. Dan Senor and Saul Singer. *Start-Up Nation: the Story of Israel's Economic Miracle* (New York: Twelve, 2009), pp. 41–54.

3. Isaiah 49:6

4. I Samuel 8:20

Chapter 2: A *Kulturkampf* Over Religion Divides Society

1. Golda Meir. *My Life* (New York: G.P. Putnam's Sons, 1975), pp. 223–24.

Chapter 3: A Bilingual State—Russian and Hebrew

1. Devorah Omer. *Rebirth—The Story of Eliezer Ben-Yehuda and the Modern Hebrew Language* (Philadelphia: Jewish Publication Society, 1972), p.44.

Chapter 5: Lifecycle Events

1. Judaism 101, http://www.jewfaq.org/birth.htm
2. Ibid.
3. Ibid., http://www.jewfaq.org/death.htm

Chapter 6: A Calendar Filled With Holidays and Holy Days

1. Hebcal Jewish Calendar, http://www.hebcal.com/

Chapter 7: Desert Factory Revives the Lost Commandment of Snail Dyeing

1. "Fringe benefits: A Kfar Adumim factory revives the lost commandment of techelet" The Jerusalem Post, In Jerusalem section, March 13, 2009, pp. 18–19.

2. Ibid.

3. Design Museum Holon, http://www.dmh.org.il/exhibition/exhibition.aspx?pid=25&catId=-1

Chapter 8: Every Day is a Feast Day in the Holy City

1. Deuteronomy 8:8

WORKS CONSULTED

Emmer, Tzuvia and Reitman, Tzipora. *Spice and Spirit: The Complete Kosher Jewish Cookbook*. New York: Lubavitch Women's Cookbook Publications, 1990.

Friedman, Tali. *The Culinary Story of Jerusalem*. Jerusalem: Morotom Publishing, 2011.

Kanotopsky, Zvi Dov. *Rejoice in Your Festivals: Penetrating Insights into Pesach, Shavuot and Sukkot*. Jerusalem: Urim Publications, 2007.

Kaufman, Sheilah. *Sephardic Israeli Cuisine*. New York: Hippocrene Books, 2002.

Meir, Golda. *My Life*. New York: G.P. Putnam's Sons, 1975.

Mishnayoth. New York: The Judaica Press, 1964.

Nathan, Joan and Goldman, Judy Stacey. *The Flavor of Jerusalem*. London: Little, Brown, 1975.

Omer, Devorah. *Rebirth—The Story of Eliezer Ben-Yehuda and the Modern Hebrew Language*. Tel Aviv: Am Oved Publishers Ltd., 2010.

Ottolenghi, Yotam and Tamimi, Sami. *Jerusalem: A Cookbook*. Berkeley: Ten Speed Press, 2011.

Senor, Dan and Singer, Saul. *Start-Up Nation: The Story of Israel's Economic Miracle*. New York: Twelve, 2009.

Sterman, Baruch and Sterman, Judy Taubes. *The Rarest Blue: The Remarkable Story of an Ancient Color Lost to History and Rediscovered*. Guilford, Conn: Globe Pequot Press, 2012.

The New English Bible. Cambridge: Cambridge University Press, 1972.

Van Creveld, Martin. *The Sword and the Olive: A Critical History of the Israeli Defense Force*. New York: Public Affairs, 1998.

FURTHER READING

Cone, Molly. *The Story of Shabbat*. New York: Harpercollins Children's Books, 2000.

Omer, Devorah. *Rebirth—The Story of Eliezer Ben-Yehuda and the Modern Hebrew Language*. Tel Aviv: Am Oved Publishers Ltd., 2010.

Sofer, Barbara. *Keeping Israel Safe: Serving the Israel Defense Forces*. Minneapolis, MN: Kar-Ben Publishing, 2008.

Waskow, Arthur O. *Seasons of Our Joy: A Modern Guide to the Jewish Holidays* (Paperback) Philadelphia: Jewish Publication Society, 2012.

ON THE INTERNET

Hebcal Jewish Calendar, http://www.hebcal.com/

The Online History Shop, http://www.historama.com

Judaism 101, http://www.jewfaq.org/

PTIL Tekhelet, http://tekhelet.com/product/rarest-blue/

Zionism & Israel Information Center, http://www.zionism-israel.com/

GLOSSARY

acronym (AK-ruh-nim)—a word formed from the initial letters or groups of letters of words

ambiguous (am-BIG-yoo-uhs)—having several meanings, not clear

ambivalence (am-BIV-uh-luhns)—uncertainty

antithesis (an-TITH-uh-sis)—opposite of

askance (ah-SKANS)—with suspicion, mistrust, or disapproval

assassinate (uh-SAS-uh-neyt)—politically motivated murder

AWOL—a military acronym for "away without official leave"

camaraderie (kah-muh-RAH-duh-ree)—French for good fellowship

chagrin (shuh-GRIN)—disappointment

circumcision (sur-kuhm-SIZH-uhn)—cutting the penis' foreskin

connoting (keh-NOHT-ing)—to signify or suggest a meaning in addition to the primary one

constitution (kon-sti-TOO-shuhn)—a country's founding laws

diaspora (DAY-as-PERR-uh)—the Jewish people living outside of Israel

fellowship (FEL-oh-ship)—community of interest

genocide (JEN-uh-sahyd)—the deliberate and systematic extermination of a national, racial, political, or cultural group

indelible (in-DEL-uh-buhl)—that cannot be eliminated, forgotten or changed

injunction (in-JUNK-shuhn)—command, mandate

Iron Curtain—the line of demarcation between Western Europe and the Soviet zone of influence following World War II

GLOSSARY

isolationist (ahy-suh-LEY-shuh-nist)—a person who favors or works for the idea of becoming separate or alone

juxtaposition (juhk-stuh-puh-ZISH-uhn)—being side by side

lexical gaps—missing words

Mimouna (mee-MOO-na)—Moroccan Jewish festival marking the end of Passover

municipal bylaw—law enacted by city hall

nascent (NEY-suhnt)—beginning to exist or develop; new

neologism (nee-OL-uh-jiz-uhm)—a newly invented word or phrase

omnipresent (om-nuh-PREZ-uhnt)—present everywhere at the same time

paeans (PEE-uhnz)—a song of praise, joy, or triumph

philologist (fi-LOL-uh-jeest)—a linguist

posthumous (pos-CHUH-muhs)—occurring after one's death

quintessential (kwin-tuh-SEN-shuhl)—the essential essence of something

rabbinic (ruh-BIN-ik)—concerning Jewish life after the Bible

raucous (RAW-kuhs)—rowdy

redundant (rih-DUHN-duhnt)—unnecessary; duplicate

secular (SEK-yuh-ler)—not connected with religion

Sigd—Ethiopian Jewish festival

statutory (STACH-oo-tawr-ee)—authorized by statute or law

synagogue (SIN-uh-gawg)—Jewish place of worship

unintelligible (uhn-in-TEL-i-juh-buhl)—not understandable

utopian (yoo-TOH-pee-uhn)—involving idealized perfection

visceral (VIS-er-uhl)—coming from instinct rather than intellect

GLOSSARY OF FOREIGN VOCABULARY

aliya (ah-lee-AH)—Hebrew for immigrating or ascending to Israel

arba kanfot (ahr-BA kan-FOT)—Hebrew for an undershirt with ritual tassels

Ashkenazi (ahsh-kuh-NAH-zi)—Hebrew for Jews of Eastern Europe and their descendants

beigeleh (bei-GE-leh)—Hebrew for an elongated, oval-shaped bread

camaraderie (kah-muh-RAH-duh-ree)—French for good fellowship

dapar efes (da-PAR e-FES)—Hebrew acronym for *dirug psychotechni rishoni* (initial psycho-technical ranking), and Efes meaning zero.

ersatz (ER-zahts)—German for synthetic or substitute

escargot (es-kar-GOH)—French for snail

Etzel (et-ZEL)—Hebrew acronym for National Military Organization, also called the Irgun

falafel (fe-LA-fel)—Arabic for balls of deep-fried chickpeas, originally from Egypt

Galgalatz (Gal-guh-LATZ)—Hebrew acronym for IDF Radio

Haganah (ha-gan-UH)—Hebrew for defense

halacha (hah-LAW-khuh)—Hebrew for Jewish religious law, literally the way

haMa'apilim (ha-ma-ah-pil-EEM)—Hebrew for the daring ones, the 80,000 clandestine immigrants who tried to slip through Great Britain's Royal Navy blockade of Palestine's Mediterranean coast prior to independence

hareidim (hah-RAY-deem)—Hebrew for ultra-Orthodox Jews, literally those who quake before God

hummus (HU-moos)—Arabic for pureed chickpeas drizzled with olive oil, originally a Lebanese dish

jachnun (jach-NOON)—Arabic for a Yemenite Jewish pastry traditionally served on Shabbat morning

kataif (ka-TAI-if)—Arabic for crescent-shaped deep-fried pancakes stuffed with cheese or walnuts and drizzled with rosewater syrup, served during Ramadan

kela shesh (ke-LA shesh)—Hebrew for Military Prison No. 6

kibbutz (ki-BOOTS)—Hebrew for ingathering, a community settlement organized under collectivist principles

kibitz (KIB-its)—Yiddish for to joke around

GLOSSARY OF FOREIGN VOCABULARY

klezmer (KLEZ-mer)—Yiddish for a style of folk music popular with Ashkenazi Jews

Knesset (kuh-NESS-et)—Hebrew for Parliament

kol ha-kavod l'Zahal (kol ha-ka-VOD l-Tza-HAL)—Hebrew for "All honor to the IDF"

knafeh nablusiya (KNA-fa na-blu-SIY-ya)—a pastry made of shredded phyllo dough, goat cheese and pistachios, originally from Nablus

kubbeh (KUB-beh)—Arabic for minced meat dumplings served in a broth

Kulturkampf (kool-TOOR-kahmpf)—German for culture struggle

kvetch (kvetch)—Yiddish word meaning to complain

l'chaim (luh-khah-YEEM)—Hebrew for a toast to life

Lehi (le-CHEE)—Hebrew acronym for Fighters for the Freedom of Israel, also called the Stern Gang

Machal (mah-CHAL)—Hebrew acronym for Overseas Volunteers, WWII veterans from across the world, mainly Jewish, who fought in Israel's War of Independence

malabi (ma-LA-bi)—Arabic for an almond pudding

megilla (me-gil-LA)—Hebrew for a scroll such as the Scroll of Esther

mesting (mes-TING)—Hebrew for mess tin

meurav yerusahalmi (me-oo-RAV ye-roo-shal-MI)—Hebrew for mixed (grill) Jerusalem (style)

Milchemet Sheshet HaYamim (mil-chem-ET shesh-SHET ha-ya-MEEM)—Hebrew for the Six-Day War, June 5-10, 1967

miluim (meh-LOO-im)—Hebrew for the IDF reserves

miluimnikim (mil-u-eem-nik-EEM)—Hebrew for those serving in the IDF reserves

Olei ha-Gardom (o-LAY ha-gar-DOM)—Hebrew, literally Those Who Ascended the Scaffold, freedom fighters hanged by the British

oy (oi)—Yiddish and Hebrew used to express dismay, pain, annoyance, grief, etc.

oznei Haman (oz-NEI ha-MAN)—Hebrew for triangle-shaped pastries stuffed with poppy seed, prunes or jam. Also called hamantaschen in Yiddish

Palmach (pal-MACH)—Hebrew acronym for Shock Troops, elite commandos of the Haganah

GLOSSARY OF FOREIGN VOCABULARY

repertoire (REP-er-twahr)—French for a list of songs

Rosh ha-Shana (rosh ha-Sha-NA)—Hebrew for the New Year, literally the head of the year

rugelach (roo-ge-LACH)—Yiddish for crescent-shaped pastries filled with chocolate, cinnamon or fruit preserves

sabich (sa-BICH)—Iraqi Arabic for an eggplant sandwich

sahlab (SAH-lab)—Turkish for a hot, gelatinous pudding-drink made from orchid tubers

Shabbat shalom (shab-BAT sha-LOM)—Hebrew greeting "Sabbath peace"

shawarma (sha-WAR-ma)—Arabic for a wrap sandwich of lamb or other meat sliced off a vertical spit, originally from Turkey

shmatta (SHMAH-tuh)—Yiddish for rag or tattered clothes

sufganiyot (soof-gan-ee-YOT)—Hebrew for jelly donuts served during Hanukah

tapuz (ta-PUZ)—Hebrew for orange, originally an acronym for golden apple

tekhelet (te-khel-ET)—Hebrew for blue dye

tisch (tish)—Yiddish for table

troubadour (TROO-buh-door)—French for a wandering singer or minstrel

tzena (tze-NAH) Hebrew for austerity, the period of food rationing after independence in 1948

tzitzit (tzi-TZIT)—Hebrew for tassels on a prayer shawl, plural tzitziot

umba (um-BAH)—Iraqi Arabic for pickled mango sauce

yeshiva (yuh-SHEE-vuh)—Yiddish for a seminary

yeshiva bochers (yuh-SHEE-vuh BOCH-ers)—Yiddish for seminary students

za'atar (za-A-tar)—Arabic for a spice blend with hyssop and oregano

Zahal (Tza-Hal)—Hebrew acronym for the Israel Defense Force, also called the IDF

INDEX

About the Author

Gil Zohar was born in Toronto, Canada, and moved to Jerusalem in 1982. He is a journalist writing for *The Jerusalem Post*, *Segula* magazine, and other publications. As well, he's a professional tour guide who likes to weave together the Holy Land's multiple narratives. Gil wrote one hundred pages of *Fodor's Guide to Israel* (7th edition, 2009) and has written tourism promotion material for Israel's Ministry of Tourism. He can be reached at GilZohar@rogers.com or +011 972 (0)524 817 482. For more information see www.GilZohar.ca.

מועצה אזורית תמר

צאתכם לשלום
Go in Peace
رافقتكم السلامة